IN THE ROOM

WHEN GRIEF COMES TO WORK

By Patricia C. Bravo

Illustrations by Dylan Terasaki

Published by Bravo For You
Seattle, WA

ISBN 979-8-9954223-0-3

Printed in the United States of America

First Edition May 2026
10 9 8 7 6 5 4 3 2 1

Written by Patricia C. Bravo

Illustrated by Dylan Terasaki

For the ones who stayed,
and for those who kept working
while their hearts were breaking.

You've found yourself in a whirlwind of grief.

Maybe you lost someone, a relationship or pet.

Or you lost a dream or future you imagined.

When we grieve, it's with us everywhere.

Including at work.

Grief comes in many sizes.

It can show up as a straight line or messy tangle.

We may carry emotional weight we don’t fully recognize.

We think we have grief under control.

Other times…it consumes us.

Through it all, we're trying to do our work.

Yet we might perform out of character.

Developing a new skill might become hard.

Leading others could conflict with needing to lead ourselves.

Sometimes our workplace supports us.

We benefit from an incredible leader.

Sometimes, our workplace is not set up to meet the moment.

It can be frustrating.

Feel unfair.

We may have to forge a temporary or new path.

We might grow and achieve differently than planned.

Our grief isn't always visible to others.

We don’t always understand it ourselves.

Yet it’s there. Adjacent to everything.

What are you carrying today?

What would bring relief?

Setting it down? Reconfiguring it?

Hurling an emotion at it? Turning it into something?

Some days you'll succeed at navigating. Some days you won't.

Workplaces can make space for grief and deepen understanding.

And so can you.

Whether you carry grief or work with someone who does...

Don’t look away from what you can’t see.

What you can’t see, may hold me.

Noticing me means I can be.

Illustrations by Dylan Terasaki

Dylan Terasaki is a Seattle-based illustrator and artist, who works across multiple mediums, including watercolor, pencil illustration, digital art and ceramics.

About the Author

Patricia C. Bravo works with leaders and teams navigating human experiences many organizations overlook. Her work helps organizations respond to unseen experiences.

If this book meets you at a meaningful moment, additional reflections and resources can be found here.

https://bravoforyou.com/in-the-room

Acknowledgments

This book was built in the company of remarkable people.

Dylan Terasaki, whose extraordinary talent gave form to what is often unseen. Your talent for working with a weighty subject is remarkable, and you brought care and form to the work, shaping its visual core. The way you translated this work, without needing to know all that sat behind it, is something I deeply admire.

Jillian Rubel, whose discernment shaped the architecture and artistic cohesion of this work. You have a rare ability to step into a piece of work, see what it is trying to become, and help bring it there. Time and again you offered exactly the right question, the right insight, the right moment of guidance. Each one strengthened the book…and me.

Hailey Whisenant, who brought discipline, research and extraordinary care to the process of bringing this book to life. Your growth alongside it and your commitment to excellence have meant so much.

Nibin Varghese, your design expertise and that of your team shaped the visual and structural integrity of the book in its final form.

Alyssa Lopez, you recognized this work early and thoughtfully offered the kind of encouragement that steadies a long creative process.

Alyssa Vindigni, your time, care and generosity in reading an early version of this work helped me see it might truly have a place in the world.

Isabel Webster-Lam, I remain grateful for the introduction that made this collaboration possible. You may never fully know the gift that was.

Beth Sauer, your artistic lens and generous critique strengthened both the work and me.

Keith Corbin, your thoughtful reflections helped refine what landed and what did not.

Renee Tynan, your constant encouragement and the way you're always in my corner means so much to me.

To my mastermind: Lisa Fain, Kore Koubourlis and Christine McHugh, your conversations, courage and candor continue to shape how I think and lead.

To my advisory teams, past and present, thank you for your openness to this work, your thoughtful engagement and your willingness to show up so readily as it began to take shape.

To A.J. Harper, whose guidance, insight and encouragement, shared through her work, have been a steady support throughout my writing process.

And to those who shared their stories of grief and trusted me with what is tender and difficult, your candor makes this work matter.

www.ingramcontent.com/pod-product-compliance
Ingram Content Group UK Ltd.
Pitfield, Milton Keynes, MK11 3LW, UK
UKHW061033310726
14089UKWH00010B/217
9798995422303